This Book
Belongs To:

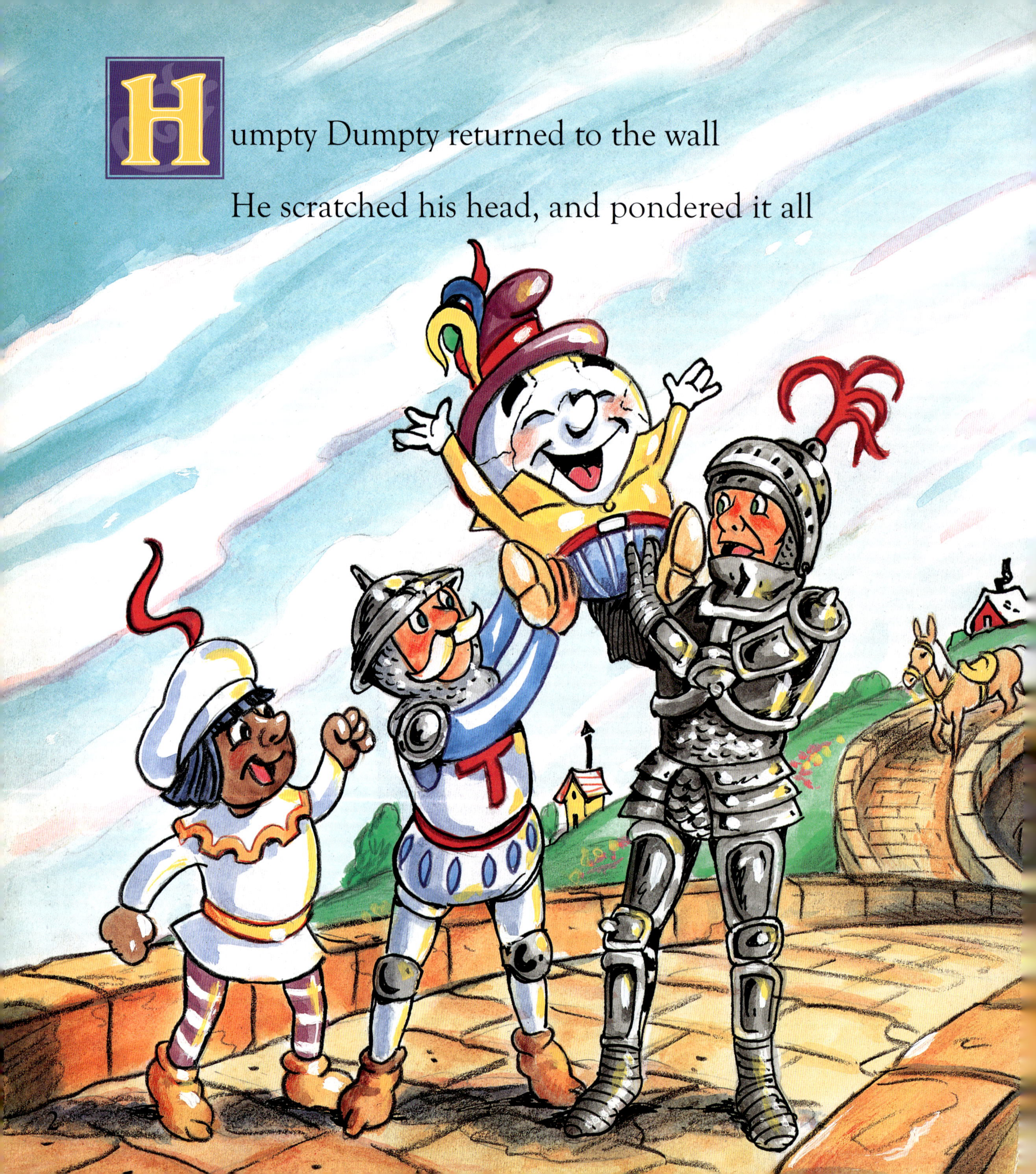
Humpty Dumpty returned to the wall
He scratched his head, and pondered it all

With the help of the horses...

And the help of the men...

Humpty Dumpty felt whole once again

Humpty Dumpty then knew in his heart

That Humpty Dumpty would play a great part

To gather with men...

And team up with horses...

He'd partner with knights, and all the good forces

AN OPEN
LETTER FROM
THE KING

To journey through life, and try to do good

And tell of the King, however he could

He'd find broken horses...

And seek injured men...

Try to heal hurts, or carry a friend

AMBULANCE

Humpty Dumpty soon walked down a street

He saw a man, who had nothing to eat

He pulled out some change...

And gave him some food...

He started to like his new attitude

Humpty Dumpty then thought of the poor

He reflected right there, "I can do even more"

'Cause all broken treasures...

No matter how cracked...

Have some sort of talent that they can give back

Humpty Dumpty then drove in his car

Determined to go, to places afar

He'd voyage by boat...

Or travel by train...

If he thought he had to, he'd fly there by plane!

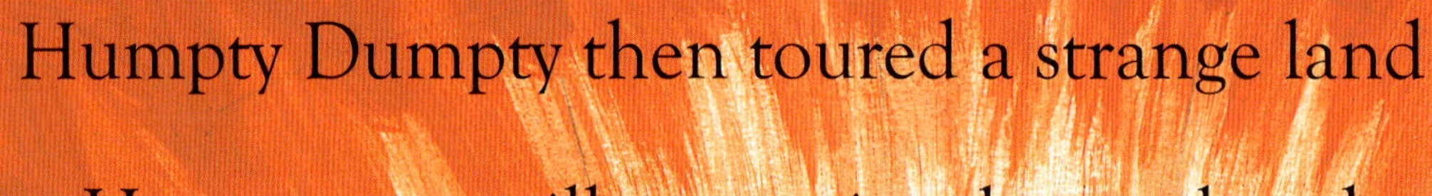

Humpty Dumpty then toured a strange land

He went to a village to give them a hand

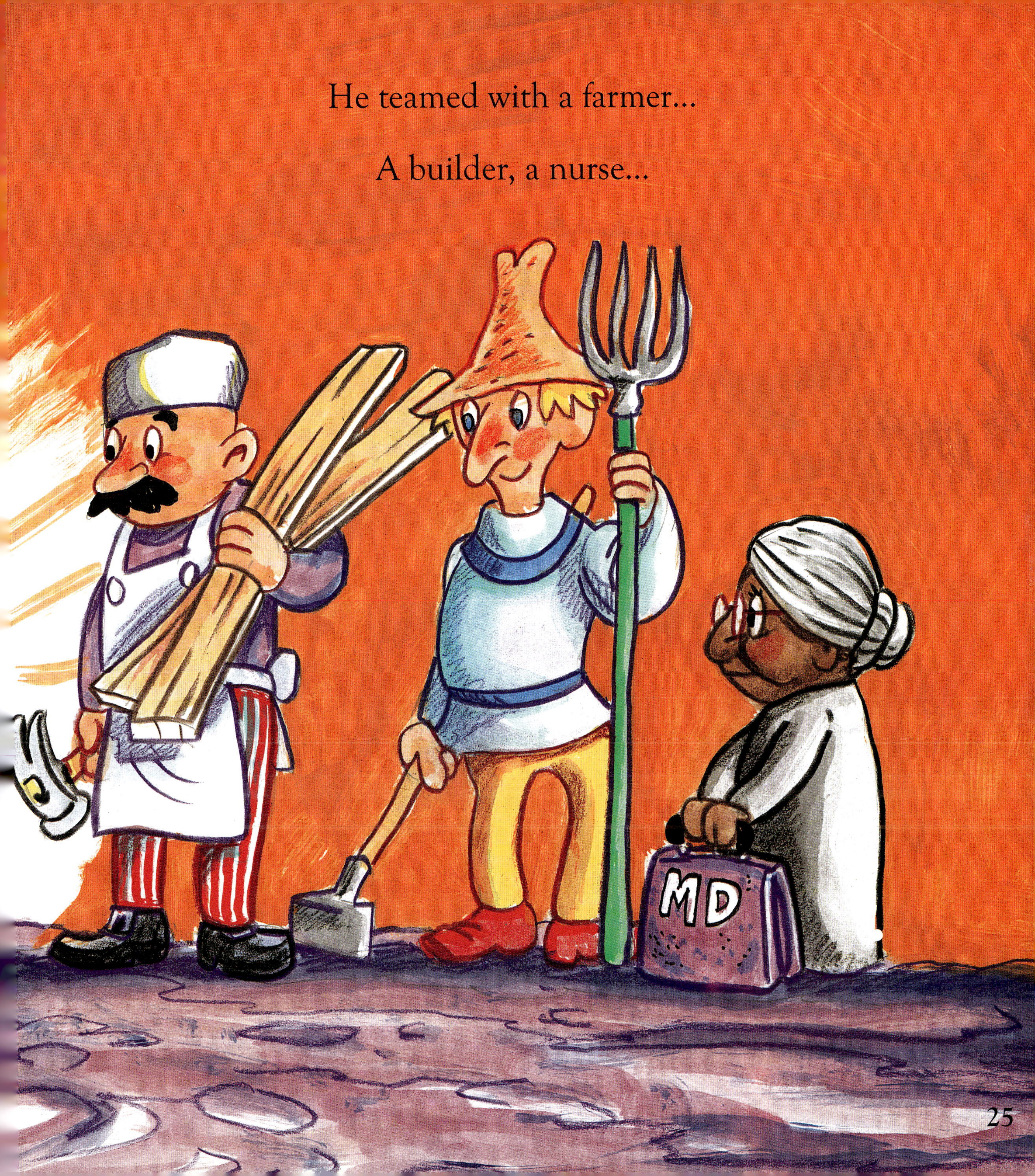

He teamed with a farmer...

A builder, a nurse...

MISSIONS
FOOD
MEDICINE

He saw lots of sickness, and hunger, and worse

But Humpty Dumpty just rolled up his sleeves

He built a new storehouse, he planted some trees

And all the strange horses...

And all the strange men...

Were ever so grateful, for a newly made friend

29

Humpty Dumpty flew home one day

Humpty Dumpty wished he could stay

He just felt so useful...

And never felt so good...

But on the way home,

he now understood

That Humpty Dumpty could travel the world
And help broken boys, and heal broken girls

But some of the treasures...
And some of the poor...